THEMATIC UNIT

OUR ENVIRONMENT

Written by Mary Ellen Sterling

Illustrated by Keith Vasconcelles

Teacher Created Materials, Inc.
P.O. Box 1040
Huntington Beach, CA 92647
©1991 Teacher Created Materials, Inc.
Made in U.S.A.

ISBN 1-55734-272-5

Table of Contents

Introduction

Our Environment contains a captivating whole language, thematic unit about the environment. Its 80 exciting pages are filled with a wide variety of lesson ideas and reproducible pages designed for use with primary children. At its core are two high-quality children's literature selections, *The Wartville Wizard* and *The Great Kapok Tree*. For these books activities are included which set the stage for reading, encourage the enjoyment of the book, and extend the concepts gained. In addition, the theme is connected to the curriculum with activities in language arts (including daily writing suggestions), math, science, social studies, art, music, and life skills (cooking, physical education, etc.). Many of these activities encourage cooperative learning. Suggestions and patterns for bulletin boards and unit management tools are additional time savers for the busy teacher. Furthermore, directions for student-created Big Books and a culminating activity, which allow students to synthesize their knowledge in order to produce products that can be shared beyond the classroom, highlight this very complete teacher resource.

This thematic unit includes:

- ☐ **literature selections** — summaries of two children's books with related lessons (complete with reproducible pages) that cross the curriculum

- ☐ **poetry** — suggested selections and lessons enabling students to write and publish their own works

- ☐ **planning guides** — suggestions for sequencing lessons each day of the unit

- ☐ **writing ideas** — daily suggestions as well as writing activities across the curriculum, including Big Books

- ☐ **bulletin board ideas** — suggestions and plans for student-created and/or interactive bulletin boards

- ☐ **homework suggestions** — extending the unit to the child's home

- ☐ **curriculum connections** — in language arts, math, science, social studies, art, music, and life skills such as cooking and physical education

- ☐ **group projects** — to foster cooperative learning

- ☐ **a culminating activity** — which requires students to synthesize their learning to produce a product or engage in an activity that can be shared with others

- ☐ **a bibliography** — suggesting additional literature and nonfiction books on the theme

---

To keep this valuable resource intact so that it can be used year after year, you may wish to punch holes in the pages and store them in a three–ring binder.

Introduction *(cont.)*

Why Whole Language?

A whole language approach involves children in using all modes of communication: reading, writing, listening, observing, illustrating, experiencing, and doing. Communication skills are interconnected and integrated into lessons that emphasize the whole of language rather than isolating its parts. The lessons revolve around selected literature. Reading is not taught as a separate subject from writing and spelling, for example. A child reads, writes (spelling appropriately for his/her level), speaks, listens, etc. in response to a literature experience introduced by the teacher. In this way, language skills grow naturally, stimulated by involvement and interest in the topic at hand.

Why Thematic Planning?

One very useful tool for implementing an integrated whole language program is thematic planning. By choosing a theme with correlating literature selections for a unit of study, a teacher can plan activities throughout the day that lead to a cohesive, in-depth study of the topic. Students will be practicing and applying their skills in meaningful contexts. Consequently, they will tend to learn and retain more. Both teachers and students will be freed from a day that is broken into unrelated segments of isolated drill and practice.

Why Cooperative Learning?

Besides academic skills and content, students need to learn social skills. No longer can this area of development be taken for granted. Students must learn to work cooperatively in groups in order to function well in modern society. Group activities should be a regular part of school life and teachers should consciously include social objectives as well as academic objectives in their planning. For example, a group working together to write a report may need to select a leader. The teacher should make clear to the students and monitor the qualities of good leader-follower group interaction just as he/she would state and monitor the academic goals of the project.

Why Big Books?

An excellent cooperative, whole language activity is the production of Big Books. Groups of students, or the whole class, can apply their language skills, content knowledge, and creativity to produce a Big Book that can become a part of the classroom library to be read and reread. These books make excellent culminating projects for sharing beyond the classroom with parents, librarians, other classes, etc. Big Books can be produced in many ways and this thematic unit book includes directions for at least one method you may choose.

The Wartville Wizard

by Don Madden

Summary

A neat and tidy old man lived on a hill overlooking Wartville. Every day he collected the trash that had been dumped on the beautiful countryside. The old man grew angrier and angrier about picking up after other people, and he delighted in calling them slobs.

One day he noticed that he had power over trash. With a point of his finger he could send trash back to the person who had thrown it. Of course, this caused quite a problem among the townspeople, and even their only doctor, Dr. Splint, could not help them.

Then Barbette happened to see the old man in action. She ran back to town to tell everyone about her discovery. Soon people were calling the old man a wizard. The townspeople gathered on his lawn and demanded that he remove their garbage. He refused to give in to their demands until they promised not to litter again. They promised, and the old man was happy once more in his neat and tidy town.

The outline below is a suggested plan for using the various activities that are presented in this unit. You should adopt these ideas to fit your own classroom situation.

Sample Plan

Day I

- Set up a garbage pool display (see page 6)
- Save that garbage! (page 6)
- Your Environment–background information (page 12)
- Trash Scavenger Hunt (page 6)
- Read *The Wartville Wizard*
- Homework Activity: Bring in garbage (page 6)

Day II

- Comprehension Activities-Sentence Strips (p. 16)
- Make Garbage Charts after sorting and measuring (page 10)
- Ecology – learn about environments (pages 20 and 21)
- Reuse It!: worksheet (page 14)

Day III

- Opposites (page 17)
- Sentence Transformations (page 18)
- Ways You Can Help (page 22)
- Make Garbage Hats (page 10)

Day IV

- Brainstorming techniques (page 13)
- Language: What If... (page 19)
- Math: Wartville Wizard's Word Problems (page 23)

Day V

- Make an Accordion Book (page 24)
- Read *Where Does The Garbage Go?*

Overview of Activities

SETTING THE STAGE

1. **Set the mood** in your classroom for an ecology unit: create a 3-dimensional bulletin board. You will need a small inflatable or plastic swimming pool and lots of trash! Be sure to clean out crumbs and rinse cans and bottles so insect pests aren't attracted to your trash site. Heap boxes, cans, newspapers, plastic and foam containers in the pool. Top the pile with a sign that asks, "What Can Be Recycled?" This display will be certain to initiate some interesting discussions and get your ecology unit off to a lively start. Directions and patterns for a more traditional bulletin board are on page 71.

What Can Be Recycled?

2. **Save that garbage!** Students may wonder how long it took you to accumulate all that trash. Turn their question into a class project and have students save their garbage for a day. At the end of the day measure how many trash cans are filled. Follow-up activities can include weighing the trash, making garbage charts (page 10), and finding out how to prepare items for recycling (see page 11).

3. **Explore** what happens to trash that is not recycled and its impact on the environment. If needed, use the Your Environment worksheet, (page 12) for background information.

4. **Homework activity.** Have the students bring in something that someone in their family was going to throw away. Brainstorm possible ways to reuse or recycle the object. (See page 13 for brainstorming techniques.) Extend the oral activity with a written one (See Reuse It! page 14).

5. **A trash scavenger hunt.** Pair students and give each pair a different list of trash items to find around school grounds. Make "ecology eyes" (see page 15) to wear on the scavenger hunt!

6. **Predict and discuss.** Tell the students you are going to read them a story titled *The Wartville Wizard* written by Don Madden. Show them the cover. Discuss the following types of questions:

   • Describe what they see. Where do they think the man is going?

   • What do they think the story is about?

   • Is the man young or old? How can they tell?

   • How do they think the man is feeling?

   • What kind of day is it? How can they tell?

   • Predict some events that might happen in the story.

Overview of Activities *(cont.)*

1. **Compare.** After you have read the story, have the children recall some of the events. How does the list compare with the predictions they made yesterday? Extend this activity with a comprehension project from page 16. The sentence strips can be used to make Big Books, test comprehension, and expand sight vocabulary.

2. **Garbage projects**. Sort and weigh the garbage before making any charts or graphs. Page 10 has two sample charts; extended weighing and measuring 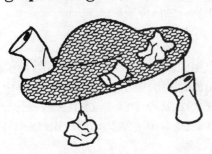 activities can be found on page 9. Two culminating trash activities include making garbage hats (page 10) and compacting the trash. For the latter, spread the trash over the classroom floor to see how much space it occupies. Challenge students to find a way to reduce the amount of space covered by the garbage. Tape around the old and new areas to give children a visual reference.

3. **Opposites.** Expand vocabulary skills and understanding of opposites (antonyms) with this activity. Choose two children to stand side by side. Have one walk slowly  and the other walk quickly. Other word pairs to pantomime include run-walk, sit-stand, up-down, over-under, happy-sad, full-empty, big-little, etc. Establish that these word pairs are opposites. Have children draw pictures of opposites or complete the worksheet on page 17.

4. **Language.** Develop language and writing skills with sentence transformations. Guidelines and samples can be found on page 18.

5. **Feelings.** Use the imaginary journey on page 13 to help students identify and describe their feelings. Further the experiment by having students wear some garbage for the day or other specified amount of time. Paper wrappers, foam containers, and other items can be taped or pinned to the students. Have them write stories about their experiences and feelings. Follow-up with the What If ? assignment on page 19.

6. **Learn about ecology.** The cut and paste activity on pages 20 and 21 explores different environments. Discuss other aspects of ecology such as recycling and conservation measures. Learn about ways they can help on page 22.

Overview of Activities *(cont.)*

ENJOYING THE BOOK *(cont.)*

7. **Math.** Practice basic math skills with the word problems on page 23. Use the page as a worksheet or as separate task cards. To make the task cards, cut apart the word problems and glue to tagboard or index cards. Laminate and place the cards in a manila envelope. Students can write on the cards with water-base pens for easy wipe-off or have students show their work on a separate sheet of paper.

EXTENDING THE BOOK

1. **Make accordion books.** Begin this activity with a brainstorming session on the events in *The Wartville Wizard*. (You may also use the Sentence Strips from page 16 as a chart from which children can copy.) To make the accordion book you will need construction paper or other paper that can be easily folded. Follow the directions on page 24 to complete a book. An alternative method for making Accordion Books is also described on the same page. Extension activities are included after each method.

    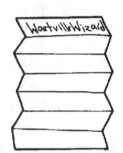

2. **Investigate what happens.** So you have all this garbage accumulated in your classroom. What do you do with it? What happens to it after you put it in the garbage pail? Find out what happens to some garbage; read *Where Does the Garbage Go?* by Paul Showers, (Crowell, 1974). Reinforce facts learned with the worksheet on page 25. Make a flow chart of the first four steps on the worksheet (see sample at right). This can be a whole group chalkboard activity or a partner seatwork activity. To make a seatwork project have students fold their sheets of construction paper into eighths. On one side write a sentence in each space. On the opposite side draw a picture to go with the text.

We put our garbage in a pail.	🗑
Trucks pick up the trash.	🚛
Trash is sent to the dump.	🚜
Dirt is put over the trash.	🚜

3. **Art.** Create art projects (see page 15) or a bird feeder (see page 26) with items from your trash collection.

4. **Get involved.** Start a trash recycling center in the school cafeteria. Make signs to hang above each trash bin - glue actual objects to a cardboard background and label with their word names.

FOOD

PLASTIC

PAPER

In the Balance

You don't need expensive equipment to weigh things. In fact, you probably have all the raw materials you'll need to build a balance right from your own trash collection! Complete directions for constructing a balance and some suggested activities are listed below.

Constructing a Balance

Materials: Metal coat hanger; string or twine; margarine cups; scissors or one-hole punch

Directions: Bend the coat hanger as shown in the diagram at right.

Attach string to the top of the coat hanger and hang it from the ceiling or some other place where it can hang freely.

Punch three evenly spaced holes in each margarine cup.

Attach a piece of string to each hole; gather all three pieces and tie a knot.

Tie the free end of the string to the coat hanger.

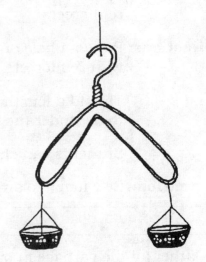

Suggested Activities

* With younger learners use non-standard units of measurement such as paper clips, bottle caps, marbles, washers, etc. to weigh pieces of trash. Record the weights on paper. Then make graphs using the information (see diagram).

* Follow up with a written exercise. Write a sentence frame on the chalkboard, chart paper, or overhead projector. Model some sentences with the students, e.g. A paper cup weighs six washers. Have students write and illustrate their own sentences.

6				
5				
4				
3				
2				
1				
cup	paper			

* Extend the activity. Compose math word problems based on the information gathered. Some examples: Which object weighs the most? the least? Choose two objects; add their weights. Subtract the smallest weight from the largest weight. Find two things that weigh the same.

* Older students can use standard units to measure. Have them find the mass in grams and weight in ounces and pounds. Make charts to compare the metric with English measurements. Learn abbreviations for ounces, pounds, grams and kilograms.

Garbage Projects

Use the garbage collected for the Homework Activity or from the day's collection of garbage to use in the following projects.

Garbage Hats

Materials: Paper plates; plastic, paper, and metal containers; scissors; white glue; yarn or string; one-hole punch; hole reinforcers

Directions: Punch a hole on either side of the plate; reinforce the holes with reinforcers.

Thread a length of yarn through the holes leaving enough to tie under the chin.

Students can choose the containers they want to attach to their hats.

Extension: Sew items to an old hat or bathing cap.

Garbage Chart

Gather all the garbage in one spot. In whole group discuss the characteristics of the trash: size, color, weight, shape, material, etc. Sort the items according to size; then sort according to color, material, shape, or weight. Divide students into groups and assign them a characteristic. Have each group make a chart of their items (see examples below and form on page 53). They can draw and cut out a sample for each item to glue to the chart, or they can attach self-stick notes to the chart. A simple bar graph could be made as a follow-up to the picture graph.

Picture Graph

Bar Graph

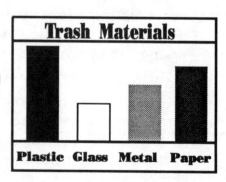

Afterwards, read the graphs. Guide students with the following questions.

• Which has the most? The least? Only one?

• How many _____ are there?

• How many more/fewer _____ than _____ are there?

• How many items are there altogether?

• How many _____ and _____ are there?

10

How to Recycle

This handy chart will show you how to prepare items for recycling.

	Glass	Separate by color (clear, brown, green). Rinse bottles and jars. Labels may be left on.
	Newspaper	Bundle with twine, or stack inside paper grocery sacks. Keep magazines and school paper separate.
	Plastic	Separate by color (clear, green). Remove the caps. Rinse out the plastic bottles and jars.
	Clothing	Wash and dry old clothes before you recycle them.
	Paper	Use both sides of your paper. Stock used paper in cardboard boxes or in paper grocery bags.
	Aluminum	Flatten them to save space. Save aluminum foil, TV dinner trays, and pie pans, too.
	Cardboard Box	Flatten the boxes. Stack them on top of one another. Tie bundles with twine.

Your Environment

All the things around you make up your environment. Some of these things are living. Some of them are not living.

Every day you live in different environments. Your classroom, your home, the movies, and the beach are different kinds of environments.

In the picture below, color all the things that are living. Circle all the things that are non-living. Draw yourself in the environment.

Brainstorming

Before you give the children a specific writing assignment, provide them with a background base from which to draw. Brainstorm words and ideas to give students a sense of what they will be writing. Record responses on chart paper, the chalkboard, or an overhead projector so that the children have a concrete reference.

Two different writing assignments are described below. Both begin with a brainstorming session.

Reuse It!

Gather some items from your garbage collection and place them on a table or desk near you. Choose one item and ask students to identify it and explain how it was used. Once that has been determined, tell the students to think of other ways they could use the same item. Ideas can be practical or creative. Write their ideas on a chart. Repeat the procedure with as many items as necessary for students to be able to complete a project on their own. Divide the students into pairs or small groups. Let them choose their own piece of trash to write about. A sample worksheet is provided on page 14, or you may direct students to fold a sheet of white construction paper in half. They can draw a picture and write in each space (see sample below).

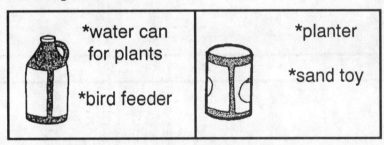

*water can for plants

*bird feeder

*planter

*sand toy

Feelings

Have students close their eyes as you take them on an imaginary journey. Tell them they have made plans to go to a water park for the end of the year party. All year long they have worked together to earn the money to attend the park. First there was a bake sale. Then they held a rummage sale. All year long they collected cans and bottles for cash. Finally, the big day arrived. Everyone piled onto the bus and sang songs until they pulled up in front of the park. A large sign was out front; it said, "Closed until further notice." Pause, and then ask the children to tell how they would feel. Record their responses on a chart. Describe another scene—one from *The Wartville Wizard.* Have students describe how they would feel if they were the wizard picking up everyone else's litter day after day, or if they were Jimmy with his whole body covered with trash. Children can work in pairs to write their feelings.

angry   scared   **upset**   *awful*   **annoyed**   *unhappy*

Name _____   *The Wartville Wizard*

Reuse It!

Work with a partner. Look through your class trash can. Choose any two pieces of trash.
Draw a picture in each box below. List all the ways you can reuse each piece of trash.

Recycled Art

Send a request letter home to parents (see page 77 for a sample) and ask them to supply egg cartons, plastic bottles, milk cartons, soda cans, and other containers they may normally throw away. Use these items to construct any or all of the art projects described below.

Art Is My Bag

- Divide the students into small groups of three or four.
- Give each group a grocery bag full of different recycled items.
- Tell the students to make a group structure using all of the things in their bag. You may want to use a kitchen timer to put a reasonable limit on this activity.
- Have the student's name and label their structures with an ecology theme.
- Rotate groups so they can view the finished products. Let them vote on the structure that best represents its theme.
- Disassemble the projects and use the containers in other activities.

Mobile of Many Uses

- Students may work on this in cooperative groups or individually.
- Allow groups to choose any container from the class collection.
- Direct them to brainstorm as many different uses for the container as they can think of. Uses may be real or humorous.
- Write each use on a separate index card.
- Attach the cards to the container with string and tape (see diagram).
- Hang up the whole container for a mobile display.

Ecology Eyes

- Direct students to make ecology glasses. They will need egg cartons, scissors, pipe cleaners, and decorative items.
- Cut egg carton cups in twos; cut the bottoms to make holes.
- Poke a hole on either side of the cup and attach a pipe cleaner to each hole. Bend the pipe cleaners to fit around the ears.

- Decorate with foil, markers, etc. Have the students wear their "ecology eyes" when they go on a trash scavenger hunt (see page 6).

Sentence Strips

Activities

1. Cut apart the sentence strips below and glue each one to a 5" x 8" (13 cm x 20 cm) index card. Place the cards in scrambled order on a chalk tray or in a pocket chart. Cards can also be given to different students. Have the students arrange the cards in correct story order.

2. Make copies of the sentence strips below. Glue each one to a separate sheet of paper. The children can work in small groups to illustrate the sentences and make Big Books.

3. Cut apart the words in each sentence. (Take care to keep each sentence separate) and glue to 3" x 5" (8 cm x 13 cm) index cards. Use with a pocket chart, a chalk tray, or a flat surface. Direct the children to put the words in correct sentence order.

Sentences

The old man saw litter in his yard.
He picked up the trash every day.
The old man grew angry.
One day he had power over trash.
Trash stuck to the person who threw it.
People did not like wearing their trash.
They met at the old man's house.
Everyone promised not to litter again.
The old man was happy.

16

Opposites

Write a word that means the **opposite.** Use the Word Bank to help you.

1. old man   ___young___   man

2. small hand   _____   hand

3. long walk   _____   walk

4. front door   _____   door

5. big barrel   _____   barrel

6. tidy house   _____   house

Challenge: On the back of this paper write sentences using the opposites and the words they describe.

WORD BANK

back   little   large

young   short   messy

Sentence Transformations

Definition

Sentence transformations involve changing some words in a sentence while leaving the structure of the sentence intact. This strategy introduces children to the process of writing more complex and interesting sentences. In the sample below, the underlined word and phrase will be changed in the new sentence that the child writes.

Original: On my way to <u>school</u> I saw <u>a boy on his bicycle</u> cross the road.

Transformation: On my way to the store I saw a woman with a grocery cart cross the road.

Several language arts skills are incorporated into this one writing activity. Sight and meaning vocabulary will be developed, specific language arts skills can be reinforced, and retention of material will be facilitated by increasing visual imagery.

Guidelines

Some guidelines for implementing sentence transformations follow.

- Choose words from the reading selections you currently use in your thematic program.

- Combine specific language arts skills with the vocabulary you choose. For example, you could focus on capitalization, use of commas in a series, etc.

- Brainstorm with the students and record their responses on chart paper, the chalkboard, or an overhead projector.

- Explain to the children the importance of drawing detailed illustrations. (It helps others know what is in their mind; the child better understands the relationship between details and main ideas.)

- For maximum quality, work on only three or four transformations in one lesson.

Samples

The following samples are taken from the *Wartville Wizard* as they lend themselves easily to transformations. Have the students fold a sheet of white construction paper in fourths; direct them to write and illustrate a different sentence in each space.

1. <u>By the mailbox</u> he saw <u>juice cans, plastic cups, and straws.</u>

2. Angry shouts and <u>grumbling noises</u> came <u>from the crowd.</u>

3. The <u>old man</u> looked at it and <u>frowned.</u>

4. As the days went by, more and more <u>townspeople</u> began <u>to wear strange outfits.</u>

5. The <u>old man</u> shook his head and <u>walked slowly</u> into the woods.

6. He opened a new <u>pack of gum</u> and carefully put the wrapper <u>in his car's litter bag.</u>

What If?

In *The Wartville Wizard* the old man could tell a piece of trash to stick to the person who threw it. If you were a character in the story, what kind of trash would you have stuck to you? Draw a picture and write a story.

Name _____

Ecology

Ecology is the study of the environment. Our world has many different kinds of environments. There are deserts, forests, oceans, and plains.

Different plants and animals live in different environments. Cut and paste the pictures below to their environments on the next page.

octopus

owl

cactus

lizard

coyote

corn

kelp

pine cone

Ecology *(cont.)*

Trace the words.

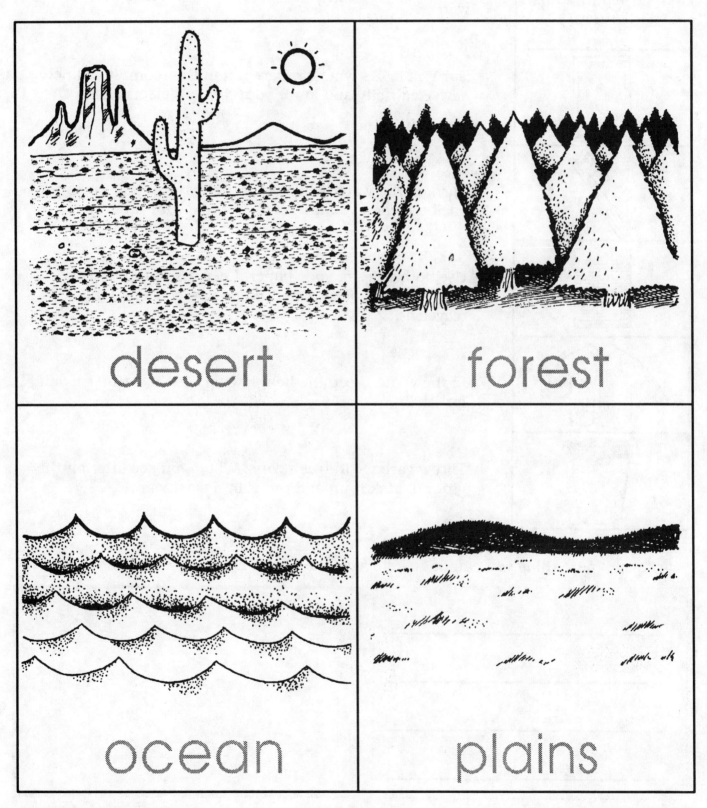

Ways You Can Help

Color the things you will do to help save the Earth.

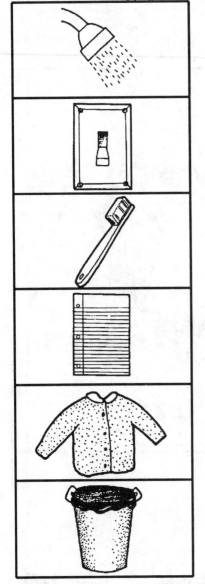

Take a short shower instead of a bath. A shower uses less water.

Turn off lights when you are not in the room. It will help save electricity and lower your family's electric bill!

Turn off the water while you brush your teeth. Turn it back on when you are ready to rinse your mouth.

Use both sides of your paper. Keep a scrap box in the classroom for used paper. When you collect enough, recycle it.

In the winter keep the heat low, put on a sweater if you feel chilly.

Throw garbage in trash cans. When you see litter on the ground, pick it up and put it in a trash can.

Write one more thing you can do to help save the Earth. Draw a picture in the box.

22

Wartville Wizard's Problems

Write a number sentence for each story. Give the answer.

1. Wizard had 8 's.

   He found 7 more.

   How many 's in all?

   _____ 's

4. Wizard picked up 3 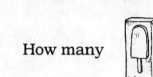 's

   He found 10 more.

   How many 's altogether?

   _____ 's

2. 9 's.

   15 's

   How many more 's?

   _____ 's

5. 9 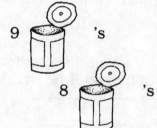 's

   8 's

   How many in all?

   _____ 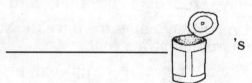 's

3. 12 's

   7 's

   How many more 's?

   _____ 's

6. Wizard found 16 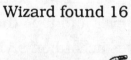 's.

   He found 7 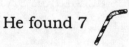 's.

   How many more 's?

   _____ 's

Accordion Books

Outlined below are two methods for making accordion books. Present these methods separately or give students a choice between the two projects. Display the accordion books on a special ecology table in the classroom or loan them to the school library for a week. That way others can benefit from and admire your class' work.

Method #1

- Each book requires one 12 x 18 inch (30 x 45 cm) sheet of construction paper.
- Beginning at one end of the paper, fold the sheet accordion-style at 3-inch (7.5 cm) intervals.
- Instruct students to write a title in the top space. Also label that space with, "Written and illustrated by."
- In each remaining space direct the students to write one or two sentences of their story.
- Have them illustrate each line.
- Accordion books can be shared in small groups.

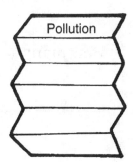

Extension:

- Have students make an accordion dictionary of environmental terms. One word and its definition should be written per line.

Method #2

- For each book you will need index cards, tape, pencil, and crayons or markers.
- Have students make a title card complete with author's and illustrator's names.
- On subsequent cards have the students write sentences for their story. They should illustrate each page.
- When the book is completed, place the index cards end-to-end with the title page at the top.
- Tape the pages together where they meet.
- Turn the pages over and tape the back seams, too.
- Fold up the pages accordion style.

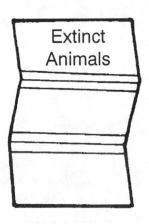

Extensions:

- Students can draw self-portraits of all the authors and illustrators of a book on the title page.
- Instead of drawing pictures, tell the students to find pictures in magazines, cut them out, and glue them to the text cards.

24

Where Does the Garbage Go?

What happens to the broken pencil you throw into the trash can at school? What about the old baseball cap you toss into the garbage at home? To find out where your garbage goes, follow the path. Trace each word. Color the pictures.

Begin

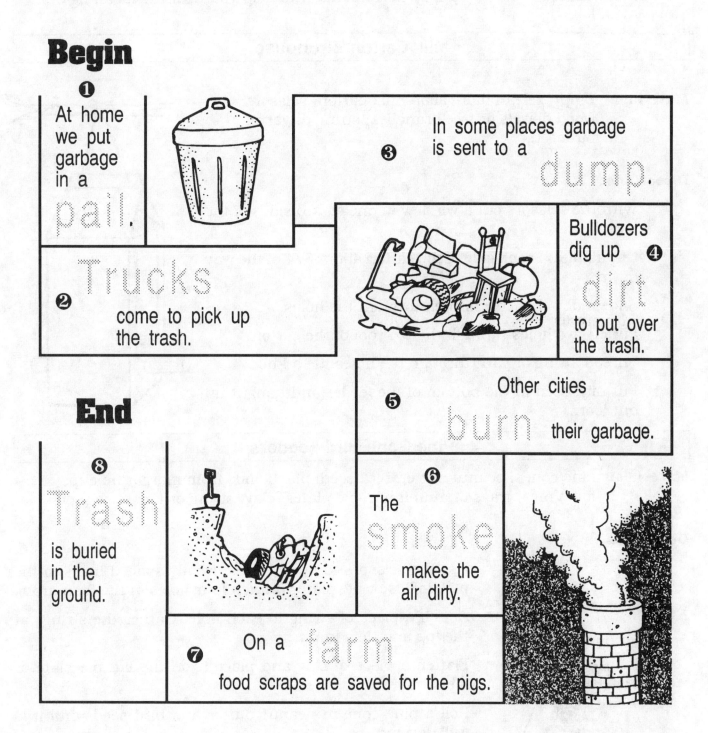

① At home we put garbage in a *pail.*

② *Trucks* come to pick up the trash.

③ In some places garbage is sent to a *dump.*

④ Bulldozers dig up *dirt* to put over the trash.

⑤ Other cities *burn* their garbage.

⑥ The *smoke* makes the air dirty.

⑦ On a *farm* food scraps are saved for the pigs.

End

⑧ *Trash* is buried in the ground.

Recycled Bird Feeders

In some cities there aren't enough trees or grasses for all the birds to build their nests. Help protect these fine-feathered friends by building a bird feeder. Not only will you be providing housing for birds, you'll be recycling too! That's called "killing two birds with one stone" (you may need an adult to help you with the meaning of this saying).

Milk Carton Birdhouse

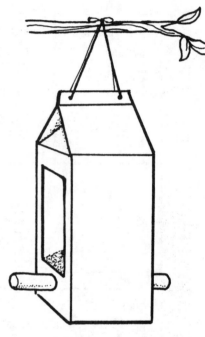

Materials: Empty, clean half-gallon milk carton; scissors; wood dowels or tree branches; string or yarn; birdseed

Directions:

* With the scissors cut a window in one or two sides of the carton.

* Cut a hole on each side of the carton about 3/4 of the way down.

* Slide a dowel or tree branch through the holes.

* Punch two holes through the top roof of the carton.

* Thread string or yarn through the holes; tie a knot.

* Put bird seed in the bottom of the feeder and hang it up outdoors.

Pine Cone Bird Feeders

Materials: Pine cones; peanut butter; bird seed; plastic lids from margarine cups; foam meat trays or aluminum pie plates; clay; string or twine; scissors

Directions:

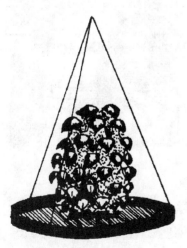

* Use the scissors to punch three evenly spaced holes in the plastic lids or pie plates (punch four holes in the foam tray).

* Attach a piece of string to each hole. Gather the strings at the top and tie a knot.

* Flatten a piece of clay and place it on the lid, pie plate or meat tray.

* Roll a pine cone in peanut butter and bird seed until it is well-covered.

* Press the pine cone onto the clay.

* Hang up the bird feeder from a tree branch outdoors.

26

The Great Kapok Tree

by Lynne Cherry

Summary

One day a man began to chop down a Kapok tree in the rain forest. It was very hot and steamy and he soon grew tired. The man sat down and before he knew it, he was asleep. One by one the animals of the forest approached the man to bring him a message. A boa constrictor was first; he told the man that the tree was his home and the home of his ancestors. "Do not chop it down," he said. Next was a bee who explained how he collected pollen. "You see, all living things depend on one another," declared the bee. Other animals followed, all imploring the man to spare the tree. When he awoke, he stood up to begin his work again. As he looked around at the animals and the beauty of the forest, he hesitated, dropped his ax, and walked out of the rain forest.

The outline below is a suggested plan for using the various activities that are presented in this unit. You should adapt these ideas to fit your own classroom situation.

Sample Plan

Day I

- Construct a Greenhouse Bulletin Board (page 31)
- Alternative: Soda Bottle Terrariums (page 32)
- Background Information on rain forests (pages 34 and 35)
- Read *The Great Kapok Tree*
- Homework (page 28)

Day II

- Homework Follow-ups (page 28)
- "Living Chart" (page 28)
- Essential Comprehension Activity: Brainstorming (page 29)
- Great Kapok Tree Puzzle (page 37)
- Rain Forest Products (page 29)

Day III

- Math. Rain Forest Facts (page 38)
- Word Bank Strategy (pages 39 & 40): Story Frames
- Poetry Writing (page 29)

- Science: Food Chain Puzzle (page 41)
- Read *Rain Forest*. Make a chart, Alike and Different (page 30)

Day IV

- Study endangered animals. Background Information, page 42.
- Make an Endangered Animals booklet (page 43)
- Writing activity: Structured Outlines (page 30)
- Rain Forest Dictionary (page 44)
- Venn Diagram (page 45)

Day V

- The Art of Henri Rousseau (page 46)
- Culminating Activity: Rain Forest Post Cards (pages 47 and 48).

Overview of Activities

SETTING THE STAGE

1. **Bulletin Board.** Ecology is much more than picking up trash and conserving water. It is also the study of communities of plants and animals that live together in various areas. So, for your second literature selection you may want to use *The Great Kapok Tree* which explores the community of the tropical rain forest. Set the stage in your classroom with a Greenhouse Bulletin Board (see page 31 for directions; diagram at right.)

    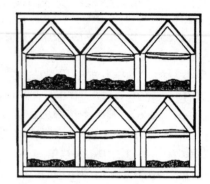

2. **Terrariums.** An alternative to the Greenhouse Bulletin Board is Soda Bottle Terrariums (see page 32 for complete directions). Small groups can work together to create their own mini rain forests.

3. **Learn about rain forests**. The cut and paste activity on pages 34 and 35 will introduce students to the layers of the rain forest and the kinds of animals that live at each level.

4. **Read *The Great Kapok Tree*.** Recall the names of the animals that spoke to the man. List them on the chalkboard or chart paper. Use the homework activity below.

5.  **Homework activity.** Direct the students to choose three animals from the list made in activity #4. Write one in each space of the Animal Favorites worksheet (page 36). Tell them to draw a picture of each one. For homework they should ask family members and people in the neighborhood to pick their favorite animal. Have the people sign their name in the proper column.

ENJOYING THE BOOK

1. **Homework follow-ups.** In small groups have the children share their homework charts. As a class, determine which animal received the most votes; the least. Find out if any animals received the same number of votes. Figure out the differences between the animal that received the most votes and the animal that received the least number of votes.

2. **Make a "living chart."** Fold masking tape over onto itself to form a giant loop. Attach it to the wall. Have each student draw and cut out a picture of their favorite rain forest animal. One at a time have them place their animal picture on the chart and explain their choice.

28

Overview of Activities *(cont.)*

ENJOYING THE BOOK

3. **Essential Comprehension Activity.** Draw a web on the chalkboard, chart paper, or overhead projector. Brainstorm events from the story and write them on the lines. Determine which animal spoke to the man first, which animal spoke second, etc. Follow up with the Great Kapok Tree puzzle on page 37. Each student may receive his own copy of the puzzle or use one puzzle for each pair of students. The teacher may also make three or four puzzles (color and cut out; glue pieces to tagboard and laminate; store each puzzle in a separate envelope) to place at a special center in the classroom.

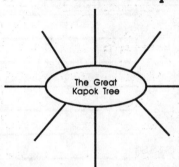

The Great Kapok Tree

4. **Explore** the reasons why the rain forest is so important to us. Brainstorm some rain forest products. Have groups of students make charts (see diagram at right) by folding a large sheet of construction paper into fourths. Write a title at the top: Rain Forest Products. Direct the groups to write a different product in each space. They may draw pictures or cut pictures from magazines and glue them onto the proper space.

Rain Forest Products	
nuts	wood
oxygen	homes for animals

5. **Math.** Learn some amazing facts about the rain forest while reviewing subtraction facts. Each student may have his own copy of this page or place copies at the class math center. Students can cover the worksheet with clear acetate and write their answers with wipe-off pens.

6. **Word Bank Strategy.** This language technique will help you maximize your Word Banks. Step-by-step directions are outlined on page 39 along with some suggested activities. Page 40 tells how to use a story frame writing with the class before letting them work independently. Encourage students to illustrate their sentences with details, including facial expressions (for more on facial expressions, see page 51).

7. **Extend the Word Banks.** Brainstorm words that rhyme with the words in the lists. Write two-line rhyming poems using words from these lists.

A lion can roar.

An eagle can soar.

Overview of Activities *(cont.)*

ENJOYING THE BOOK

1. **Learn about the food chain.** Have students put together a Food Chain Puzzle (page 41). Brainstorm lists of other meat-eaters, plant-eaters, plants, and decomposers. Tell students to draw their own food chain using a flow chart format (see diagram at right).

```
┌─────────────────┐
│   Food Chain    │
└─────────────────┘
         │
         ▼
┌─────────────────┐
│                 │
└─────────────────┘
         │
         ▼
┌─────────────────┐
│                 │
└─────────────────┘
         │
         ▼
┌─────────────────┐
│                 │
└─────────────────┘
```

Alike	Different
*are about the rain forest	*one man tries to chop a Kapok tree
*have colorful pictures	*bulldozer comes to cut trees
*animals are in danger	

2. **Read *Rain Forest*** by Helen Coucher (Farrar, Straus and Giroux, New York, 1988). Discuss how it is similar to and different from *The Great Kapok Tree*. Divide the students into small groups and direct the groups to make charts of likenesses and differences. They may illustrate their sentences. **Note:** Another excellent follow-up story is *Where the Forest Meets the Sea* by Jeannie Baker (Greenwillow Books, 1987).

3. **Study endangered animals.** Some good nonfiction books are *Animals in Danger, Endangered Animals,* and *Sticker Book of Wild Animals* (see Bibliography page 80 for more information). Students can do the worksheet on page 42 and then make their own Endangered Animals book from page 43. Direct them to color and then fold together (keep page 1 facing you while you fold.) Extend the activity with a structured outline; have students fill in the blanks and illustrate their sentences. Model some sentences with students before giving them this assignment.

Structured Outline

The _____ is endangered because_____.

---

4. **On-going dictionary.** Start students off with the Rain Forest Dictionary (page 44). As the unit progresses they can add new words to their dictionaries.

5. **Make a Venn diagram** comparing two rain forest animals. See page 45 for a sample.

6. **Art.** Henri Rousseau painted jungle scenes although he never actually visited a jungle! Learn about him and his art (see page 46).

7. **Big Book idea.** Write Rain Forest Post Cards. Directions and patterns can be found on pages 47 and 48.

Greenhouse Bulletin Board

This stunning display is sure to captivate student interest! Although it looks best on windows, the Greenhouse Bulletin Board can also be built on a regular bulletin board background. **Note:** Make sure that you build this display in a place where it will receive some sunlight.

Materials: Masking tape or paper strips; self-sealing, plastic sandwich bags; potting soil; seeds; water

Directions:

- On the window, classroom door, or bulletin board, outline a grid with masking tape or paper strips (see diagram at right).

- Give each student a self-sealing plastic sandwich bag.

- Fill the bags about one-fourth full with soil.

- Sprinkle seeds (mustard, watercress, and birdseed germinate quickly) onto the soil.

- Add just enough water to moisten the soil (do not overwater!) before sealing the plastic bags.

- Write student names on masking tape and label the bags.

- With masking tape attach one bag per section to the greenhouse.

Activities:

- Observe the seeds daily. Keep written records (use Changes worksheet page 33), drawings, or tape recordings of changes.

- Make two greenhouses—one in sunlight and one in a dark area of the classroom. Predict which ones will grow best; compare the actual growth of seeds in both groups.

- Once the seeds have sprouted, you may want to transfer them to a regular planter. Sort through your trash collection to find appropriate containers: tin cans, plastic soda bottles and margarine cups, foam cups, etc.

Extension:

- Make your own planters. You will need flour, salt, water, mixing bowl, shellac, paint brush, and an ice cream stick or plastic spoon.

Directions:

In mixing bowl combine four parts flour, one part salt, and 1 1/2 parts water. Blend well with hands. Shape the dough into a small pot. With ice cream stick or plastic spoon draw designs on the outside of the pot. Punch a drainage hole in the bottom of the planter. Bake at 350°F (180°C) for one hour. Cool completely; paint it inside and out with shellac.

Soda Bottle Terrarium

Students can make their own mini-environments with plastic soda bottles, seeds, and small plants. Other materials and the directions are listed below. Small groups may work together on one terrarium or students can build their own individual gardens.

Note: The directions below can be copied and placed at a special center where all the necessary materials and equipment are available. Make a chart and assign center times to the students.

How to Make a Soda Bottle Terrarium

You will need: 1 plastic soda bottle with top cut off

potting soil

grass seed

small plants

gravel

water

spoon

plastic wrap

rubber band

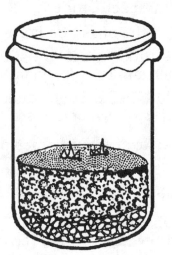

What to do:

- Make a layer of gravel on the bottom of the bottle.
- Spoon the soil into the bottle; fill it about 1/3 full (see picture above).
- Sprinkle the grass seed on top of the soil.
- Poke a hole in the soil with your finger.
- Put the roots of the plant into the hole.
- Smooth the dirt in and around the hole.
- Water the plants lightly.
- Cover the top of the bottle with plastic wrap.
- Place a rubber band around the plastic wrap to keep it in place.

Follow-up:

- Draw a picture of your terrarium. Label it Day One.
- Observe your garden every day of the week. Draw a picture of any changes you see. Label each change with the day. Use the Changes worksheet (page 33) for your work.

Changes

In each box draw a picture of the changes you observe. Be sure to write the day and date in each box.

Day 1 **Date:**_____	**Day** ___ **Date:** _____
Day ___ **Date:** _____	**Day** ___ **Date:** _____
Day ___ **Date:** _____	**Day** ___ **Date:** _____

Rain Forest Animals

A rain forest has four layers—the top layer, umbrella, understory, and floor. Different animals live in each layer. Color, cut out, and glue the animals below to the correct layer of the rain forest on the next page.

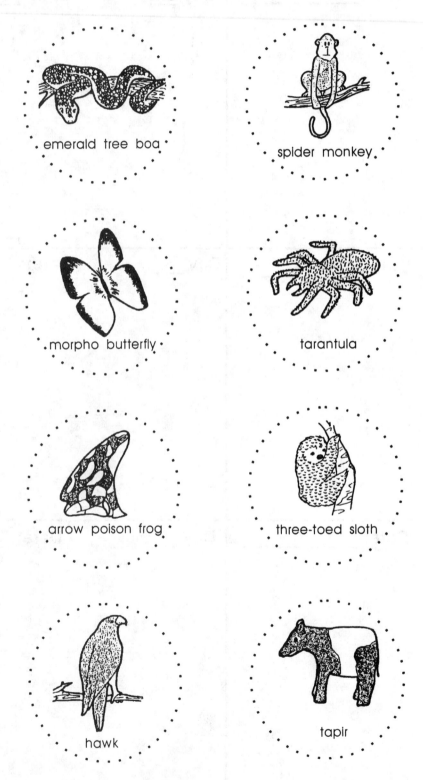

34

Rain Forest Animals *(cont.)*

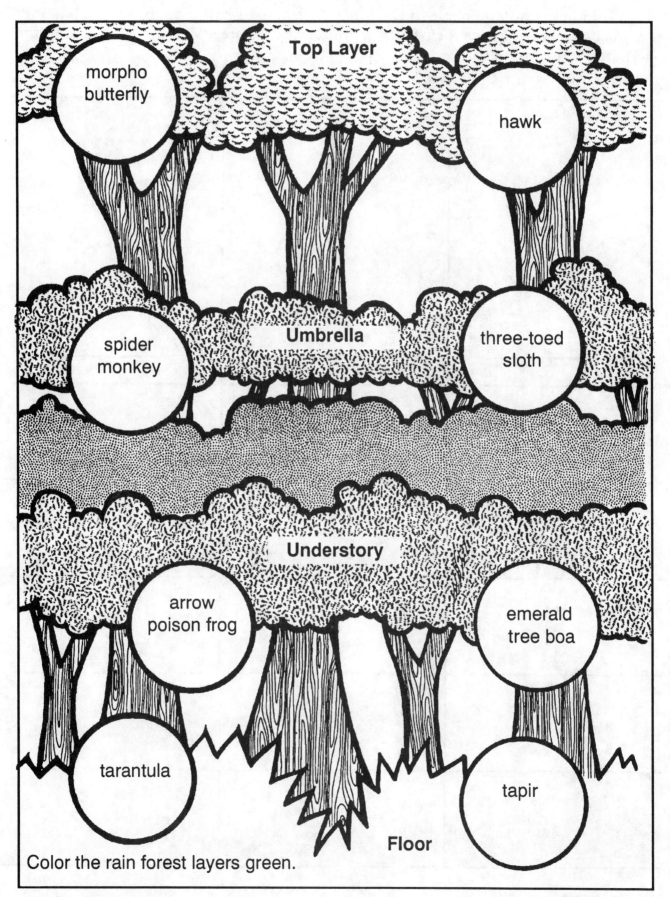

Color the rain forest layers green.

Animal Favorites

Write a rain forest animal name in each numbered box. Draw a picture of each animal there. Ask others to choose their favorite animal of the three. Write their names in the spaces below the animal.

1	**2**	**3**
_____	_____	_____

Great Kapok Tree Puzzle

4. Color.

3. Glue to paper.

2. Sequence.

1. Cut out.

6. The jaguar wouldn't be able to find dinner.

4. The toucan told how people cleared the land.

1. The boa said the tree was his home.

9. The three-toed sloth wouldn't be able to find dinner.

5. The frog told how he would be homeless.

2. The bee told how he gets pollen.

8. Some anteaters told of a world without trees.

3. Monkeys said the soil would wash away.

7. Four porcupines said trees produce oxygen.

Rain Forest Facts

Solve each problem. Write the answer in the box. Then read the amazing rain forest facts.

1. $11 - 3 =$ A tropical rain forest receives 4 to [ ] meters of rain per year. That's higher than a two-story building.

2. $7 - 5 =$ Trees in a rain forest grow roots above ground because only [ ] inches of soil have food for plants.

3. $9 - 3 =$ Hercules beetles can grow to 5 or [ ] inches long. They look like knights in armor with their large pincers and heavy shells.

4. $11 - 8 =$ This sloth has only [ ] toes. It crawls upside down on tree branches.

5. $10 - 5 =$ Toucans have [ ]-inch beaks which are almost as long as their bodies!

6. $9 - 5 =$ Rain forests have [ ] main layers. Different animals live in each layer.

7. $8 - 6 =$ A spider monkey's body is only [ ] feet long, but its tail is even longer!

8. $12 - 2 =$ Some trees grow to be [ ] meters thick. That's as wide as 6 cars placed side by side.

38

Word Bank Strategy

Try this brainstorming technique to maximize your word banks. Record the children's responses on a chart (see sample below). Keep the chart on display for students to refer to when they do writing activities.

How To

* Choose a specific topic, e.g. rain forest animals.

* Ask five questions about the topic.

   1. What are the names of some rain forest animals?

   2. What do the rain forest animals do?

   3. Where do the rain forest animals live?

   4. What do rain forests animals eat?

   5. What sounds do rain forest animals make?

* Make a chart with one or two-word headings taken from each question (see sample chart below). Ask one question at a time and list student responses in the appropriate column.

Suggested Activities

* Direct students to write a story using one word from each column. Challenge your better writers to use two or three words from each column.

* Give students a story frame; let them choose words from the Word Bank to write in the blanks.

* Write some words from the Word Bank on rectangular cards. Use for pocket chart activities.

Sample Chart

Rain Forest Animals

names	do	live	eat	sounds
boa constrictor	slither	in tree tops	insects	roar
three-toed sloth	collect pollen	in tree trunks	small animals	hoot
	climb	underground	leaves	hiss
anteater	crawl	on the sloth	ants	screech

Word Bank Strategy *(cont.)*

Story Frame

* Write a sample story frame on the chalkboard, chart paper, or overhead projector.

* Model with the students how to choose words from the Word Bank to fit into the frame.

* Direct students to copy the story frame onto a sheet of paper; tell them to leave room for the words they are going to write in the spaces.

* After the students have written words in their spaces, they may illustrate their story.

* Encourage them to share their story with their classmates, parents, and other family members.

* In some cases you may want to supply the child with a pre-written story frame. Duplicate the story frame below as many times as needed.

_____
title

Written and illustrated by :_____

The_____

is a rain forest animal. It lives

_____

and eats_____.

A_____ can

_____and_____.

40

A Food Chain Puzzle

Learn about the Food Chain. Cut out the puzzle pieces below. Glue the pieces together onto a sheet of construction paper. Color the pictures.

1. Decomposers turn waste into "food" for plants.

2. Green plants use food from the ground to grow.

3. Plant Eaters become food for meat eaters.

4. Meat Eaters make waste for the decomposers to use.

Endangered Animals

Nearly 800 different kinds of animals around the world are endangered. Endangered means that they are in danger of becoming extinct. When all the animals of a kind die and there are no more left to make babies, they are extinct.

Learn more about endangered animals. Color the animals below. Read the sentences to learn how they become extinct.

Brown Bear
Some farmers shoot brown bears to keep them away from the farm animals.

Orang-utan
People are cutting down the trees where orang-utans live to make space for new homes. The trees grow food for the orang-utans.

Tiger
This big cat is killed for sport and for its fur. Its fur is used to make coats and rugs.

Garter Snake
The marshes where the San Francisco garter snakes live are being drained to build towns.

Bald Eagle
Factories wash poisons into the oceans. Fish and small animals swallow the poisons. Then, the bald eagle eats the poisoned fish and dies.

Some Endangered Animals

Fold first.

1. The rhinoceros is hunted for its horn. Some people believe the horn can be used to make medicine.

2. Leopards are hunted for sport and for their fur. They live in Asia and Africa.

3. An orang-utan is a big red-haired ape. Its home is the rain forest trees which are being destroyed.

4. Ospreys are in danger because their food is being poisoned. Some factories dump poisons into rivers and oceans where fish swallow these poisons.

Rain Forest Dictionary

Make your own rain forest dictionary. Cut out the boxes. In each box write what the word means. Draw a picture. Put the pages in ABC order. Staple the pages together with the cover on top.

My Rain Forest Dictionary by _____	**equator**
rain forest	**understory**
canopy	**layers**

44

Name _____

Tiger and Sloth Venn Diagram

Compare the three-toed sloth with the bengal tiger. Write the words in the correct spaces.

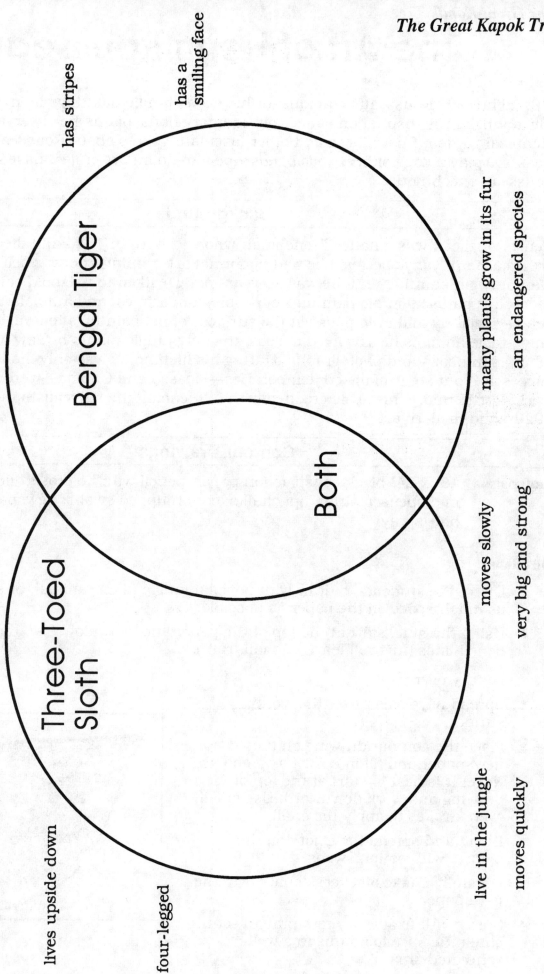

has stripes

has a smiling face

many plants grow in its fur

an endangered species

Bengal Tiger

Both

Three-Toed Sloth

moves slowly

very big and strong

lives upside down

four-legged

live in the jungle

moves quickly

45

The Art of Henri Rousseau

Although Henri Rousseau is famous for his exotic jungle paintings he never actually saw a jungle! His inspiration came from ordinary houseplants he observed in a botanical garden. Share these and other fascinating facts about Rousseau with the class. Display a copy of his *Exotic Landscape* and do an art project based on Rousseau's technique.

Background

Henri Rousseau was a native Frenchman who was born in 1844 and died in 1910. His art is called *primitive* because he had no formal art training and was self-taught. Henri did not begin painting until he was 40 years old. He liked to use bold colors and decorative patterns in his paintings of people, landscapes, and animals. He portrayed details precisely and even polished the surfaces of his paintings to a high gloss! The only jungle animals he saw lived in zoos; the only jungle plants he saw were ones from pictures in books and photographs. During his lifetime he was only moderately successful, but some of his contemporaries—Picasso and Gaugin—were admirers of his work. Furthermore, his art is credited with influencing the surrealism movement of the 1920's and modern art.

Contour Drawings

Materials: 18" x 24" black construction paper; pencil with no eraser; liquid white glue in dispenser with a tip; chalks; cotton tipped swabs; newspaper; fixative or hair spray

Directions:

- Direct the students to draw with pencil a jungle plant, animal, or scene filling up as much space on the paper as possible.

- Using the glue, start at the top of the paper and work down, as they go over the pencil lines (this will leave a "snail trail").

- Let dry overnight.

- Spread newspaper over the working surface.

- Place the contour drawing on the newspaper and fill in color using chalks. **Note:** It is best to start at the top of the drawing and work downward. Use small, even strokes to apply the chalk.

- Blend and spread the colors on the picture with cotton swabs.

- Carefully shake off excess chalk over the newspaper.

- Spray with fixative or hairspray to set the chalk. Be sure to do this in a well-ventilated area!

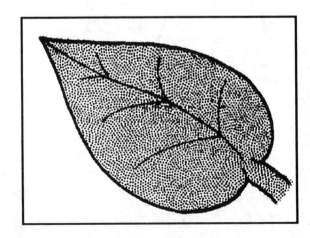

Post Cards From the Rain Forest

This project is designed to instill in youngsters an appreciation for the rain forest of our world and to alert them to the dangers that presently face these areas. First, teach the children about the importance of the rain forest (Rain Forest Facts worksheet, page 38, can be used for some background information). Then discuss some things they can do to help protect the rain forests. (*50 Simple Things Kids Can Do to Save the Earth* by the Earth Works Group is a great resource for this activity.) List the things on a chart, an overhead projector, or the chalkboard. Children can use this list when they write their post cards.

Making the Post Cards

- Duplicate the post card on page 48; make one for each student.

- On the front of the post cards, have the students draw a picture of an insect, plant, or animal in the rain forest. The children can also cut out pictures from magazines to make a rain forest collage; pictures are then glued to the front of the post card.

- Brainstorm lists of rain forest insects, plants, and animals. Next to each word write at least one way that insect, plant, or animal is important to the rain forest.

- Tell the students to choose one topic from the list above. On the front of the post card write one or two sentences explaining who they are and why they are important to the rain forest. (You may want to model this for the students before they begin to write their own sentences. See the sample below.)

- Now have the students address their post cards to someone they know or to their Congressman or even the President or Prime Minister!

- Finally, direct them to design their own stamp.

- Finished post cards can be displayed in a specially decorated shoe box; actually sent to the addressee; or if all post cards are written to the same person, mailed together in a large manila envelope.

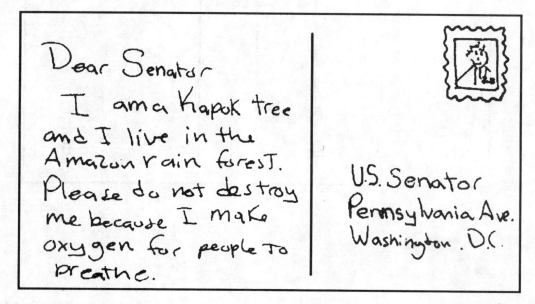

Dear Senator
I am a Kapok tree and I live in the Amazon rain forest. Please do not destroy me because I make oxygen for people to breathe.

U.S. Senator
Pennsylvania Ave.
Washington. D.C.

Post Card

Duplicate onto heavy white paper or construction paper.

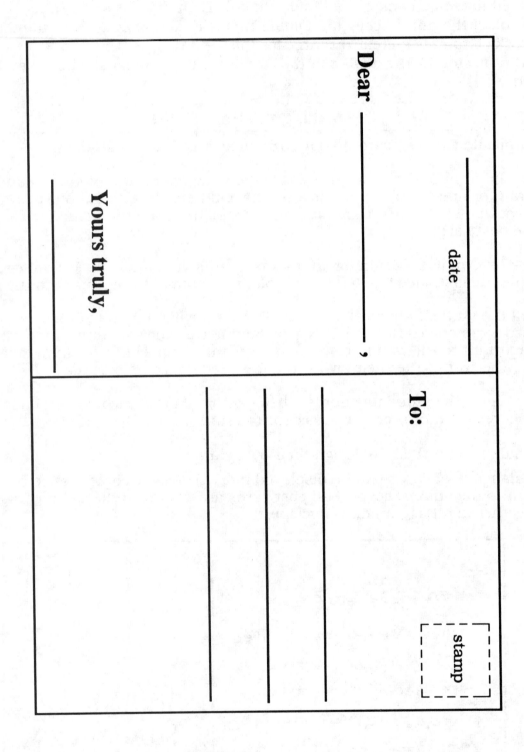

48

Things to Know Crossword Puzzle

Read each sentence below. Write the **bold** words in the crossword puzzle.

ACROSS

2. We get **oxygen** to breathe from trees and plants.

3. **Litter** can be harmful to animals.

7. Oil, paint, and gasoline are **toxic** and should not be dumped on the ground.

8. Cars, trucks, and buses **pollute** the air we breathe.

DOWN

1. Some animals have become **extinct** because they were hunted too much.

4. The **umbrella** layer of the rain forest gets a lot of sunlight.

5. You can **recycle** your old clothes and toys.

6. **Ecology** is the study of the environment.

Ecology Word Bank

These are some words you may know or want to know from your environment unit. Add new words to the list as you learn about them.

ecology	pollute
environment	energy-efficient
food chain	smog
water cycle	conserve
poisons	litter
acid rain	wastes
recycle	toxic
biodegradable	precycle
extinct	rain forest
endangered species	oxygen
carbon dioxide	

Facial Expressions Chart

Display this chart to give students a visual reference for facial expressions they may want to draw to illustrate their sentences. Add to the chart as new words are added to their vocabulary. (Refer to page 29 for details.)

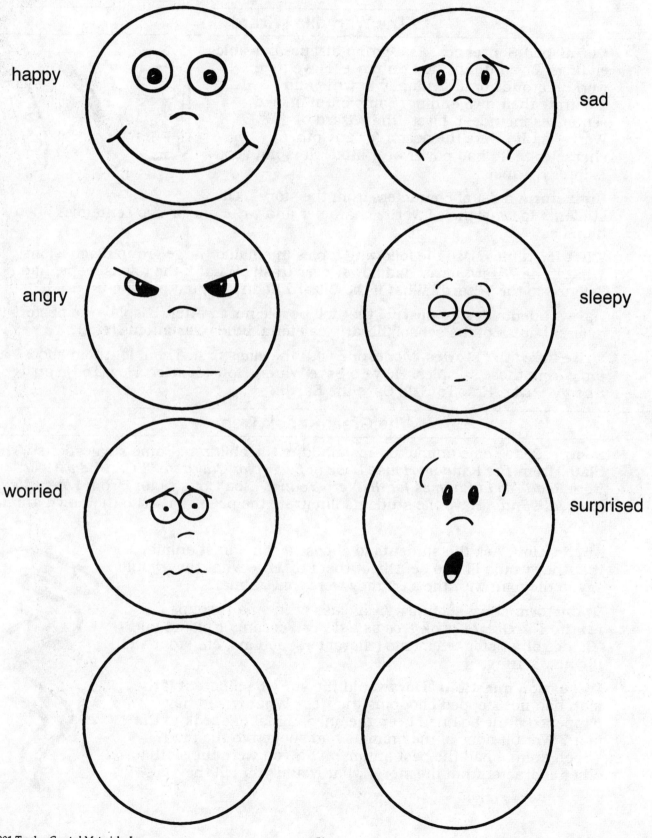

happy

sad

angry

sleepy

worried

surprised

Language Activities

The following ideas can be used anytime during the environment unit. Some activities can be completed cooperatively in small groups. Other assignments may be better suited for individual completion.

The Wartville Wizard

- **Unfinished Sentences.** As a group discuss possible endings for an unfinished sentence. Have them work in groups or individually to write and illustrate their own ending. Sample unfinished sentences include: If I were the Wizard of Wartville...If I were the doctor (or any other character)... If I had power over litter...It is not good to litter because...

- **Brainstorm** a list of characters from the story. Tell students to draw their favorite character and write one or two sentences about him/her.

- **What If? topics.** Use the following topics in small or large group discussions: What if the Wizard never had power over trash? What if the townspeople had not listened to the Wizard? What if the Wizard hadn't started picking up trash?

- Have students **design posters** that tell people not to litter. Display the posters in different areas of the school (library, cafeteria, other classrooms, etc.).

- **Write "how to" stories.** Model one with the class first. Then, let them choose a topic from these samples: How To Save Water; How to Litter; How To Be an Energy-Saver; How To Help Save the Earth.

The Great Kapok Tree

- **Poetry.** Read some animal poems aloud to the children. Some suggestions: "The Sloth" from *The Random House Book of Poetry for Children*; "I Can Be a Tiger" from *Read-Aloud Rhymes for the Very Young*; "Boa Constrictor" from *Where the Sidewalk Ends*. Have the students illustrate the poems or write their own animal poetry.

- **Application.** Ask the students to choose a rain forest animal that they would like to be. Direct them to write what they would say to the man with the ax if they were that animal.

- **Brainstorm story settings.** As a class or in small groups rewrite *The Great Kapok Tree* as a desert, ocean, or plains tale. Change other story elements (characters, actions, etc.) to match the new setting.

- **Discussion questions.** How would the story be different if the man had not stopped chopping the tree? What would have happened if the boa had been the only animal to speak to the man? What if none of the animals had spoken to the man? Which animal had the best argument? If you were the sloth (or other character from the story) what would you tell the man?

52

Graph

Write a name for the graph.

Draw pictures or write words in the boxes.

10 9 8 7 6 5 4 3 2 1

Name _____

Animal Math

Count. Write a number sentence.

1

4 + 3 = 7

2

_____

3

_____

4

_____

5

_____

6

_____

54

Who Am I?

Read the clues. Write the name of the animal. Use the Word Bank to help you.

1. One of my eyes looks forward while the other one looks back. I can also change my color.

    _ h _ _ _ _ e _ _

2. I am very big and intelligent, gentle and shy. I am a plant-eater.

    _ _ r _ _ _ a

3. My color helps me hide in my environment. I eat my prey whole.

    _ y _ _ _ _

4. Many tiny plants grow in my fur. I move very, very slowly.

    _ _ o _ _

5. I live high in the branches of the rain forest. I use my long tail as a whip.

    _ g _ _ n _

6. My stripes hide me in the grass and bamboo. I am becoming very rare.

    _ i _ _ _

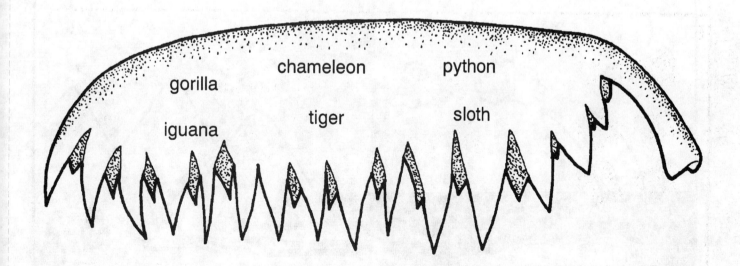

gorilla   chameleon   python

iguana   tiger   sloth

Name _____   *Science*

The Water Cycle

The Earth uses the same water over and over! Follow the flow chart to find out how.

Begin

1. **The sun evaporates water from the oceans.**

2. **The water condenses and forms clouds.**

3. **Precipitation falls from the clouds.**

4. **Water flows back to the ocean.**

Below is a picture of the water cycle. Trace the words.

Spot the Animal

With a brown crayon, color each space that has one dot in it. You will find an endangered animal.

With a green crayon, color each space that has two dots in it. You will find where the animal lives.

Trace the word.

I am a koala.

Science

Ecology Experiments

Save Water

Help the children visualize how much water is wasted when they wash their hands or brush their teeth. Afterwards, they can teach their families how to save water.

Materials: Clean, empty milk cartons; access to running water; toothbrushes; soap; towels

Directions:

- Have the students work in pairs.
- One child waters and soaps his hands. As he is doing this, the other child collects the running water in the milk carton. Have the second child remove the milk carton while the first child rinses his hands.
- The same procedure can be followed when brushing teeth.

Discussion:

How much water was collected? (Place the milk cartons side by side or empty all of them into a large container.) Tell students to think about their family members and all the times they wash their hands or brush their teeth in one day. Now imagine all the families in the class and the water they waste. Is it a lot? Can they imagine how much water is wasted by everyone in the city, state, country, or world? What could they do with the water they collected? How could they save water when washing their hands or brushing their teeth? Suggest that they show and tell their own families how to turn off the water until they need to rinse.

Make It Rot

Students will be able to see for themselves what is and is not biodegradable. Furthermore, they will gain a greater appreciation of the effects of trash on our environment.

Materials: Clear plastic storage jar with lid (one per group); one piece of trash from each category (non-meat food scraps, leaves, glass, wood, paper, plastic, cloth, and metal); soil; water

Directions:

- Divide the students into small groups and provide each group with the supplies listed above.
- Direct each group to fill their plastic jar with the trash and soil; add water.
- Put the lid on tightly and observe the changes that take place.

Discussion:

Predict what will happen to the different pieces of trash. Make group charts to show which items will rot and which will not rot. Place some containers in sunlight and some containers in a dark spot. What effect will light have on the decaying process? Keep checking the chamber monthly. If the students want to open the container to examine the contents more closely, tell them to wear rubber gloves.

An Important Message

Write the letter that comes next to find Smokey Bear's message. Color the pictures.

$\underline{\quad}$ $\underline{\quad}$ $\underline{\quad}$ $\underline{\quad}$ **you**
 n   m   k   x

can $\underline{\quad}$ $\underline{\quad}$ $\underline{\quad}$ $\underline{\quad}$ $\underline{\quad}$ $\underline{\quad}$ $\underline{\quad}$
         o   q   d   u   d   m   s

$\underline{\quad}$ $\underline{\quad}$ $\underline{\quad}$ $\underline{\quad}$ $\underline{\quad}$ $\underline{\quad}$
 e   n   q   d   r   s

$\underline{\quad}$ $\underline{\quad}$ $\underline{\quad}$ $\underline{\quad}$ $\underline{\quad}$!
 e   h   q   d   r

More Topics

Some topics related to ecology are listed below. You may wish to incorporate them into your unit of studies.

Forest Service

This agency is part of the United States Department of Agriculture. Its job is to promote the best use of forestland and to protect the forests from fire, disease, and insects. Forest Service Rangers preserve wildlife and supervise camping and picnic areas. Students can send away for their own Junior Forest Ranger Kit by writing to: Smokey Bear, c/o Smokey Bear Headquarters, Washington, D.C. 20252. Make sure they include their name and address in their request letters.

Smokey Bear

Smokey Bear was created in 1950, to promote forest awareness among young children. Smokey appeared on posters and television ads for many years. His slogan was, "Only you can prevent forest fires." Have your students work in pairs to complete Smokey's puzzle (page 59).

Woodsy Owl

After the Smokey Bear campaign, Woodsy Owl was introduced as the spokesperson for the Forest Service. His slogan was, "Give a hoot. Don't pollute!" Challenge your students to create their own anti-pollution slogan. Have them make bumper stickers for cars.

National Wildlife Federation

The National Wildlife Federation publishes two excellent nature magazines for children—*Your Big Backyard* and *Ranger Rick*. *Your Big Backyard* is appropriate for preschoolers (three to five year olds) and is complete with parent directions. It is composed of 36 issues during a 3-year period. Children aged six to twelve will enjoy *Ranger Rick*, a monthly publication.

For more information, write to:

**National Wildlife Federation
1400 16th Street, N.W.
Washington, D.C. 20077-9964**

60

Find the Way

Help the monkey find a safe path to the banana plant. Draw lines and color as you go.

START

1. Go south. Color the rocks gray.

4. Go west. Color the bananas green.

END

3. Go north. Color the bridge red.

2. Go east. Color the grapevine brown.

Where in the World?

There are many rain forests in the world. *The Great Kapok Tree* tells a story about the rain forest in the Amazon. Find the Amazon River on the map below. Color the area around it rain forest green.

Have your teacher help you find where you live on the map. Make a blue X on the spot. Draw a red line from your home to the rain forest of the Amazon.

Learn About the Author/Illustrator

Don Madden (1927-)

Artist and author Don Madden attended school at what is now the Philadelphia College of Art. He has worked as a free-lance illustrator for magazines, books, and advertising. Some of his art has appeared in *Good Housekeeping* and *Seventeen* magazines. Mr. Madden has received three gold medals from the Philadelphia Art Director's Club for his artwork.

Much of his work is done in watercolor and pen and ink with touches of chalk. Don's whimsical humor shines throughout his drawings and story of the *Wartville Wizard*.

Lynne Cherry (1952-)

Lynne Cherry is a career illustrator and a children's author. She attended art school in Philadelphia, Pennsylvania and began her career as a paste-up artist and designer in Bronx, New York. Ms. Cherry has illustrated magazines, newspapers, and retail advertising and has designed numerous calendars and note cards. Her outstanding illustrations for *The Snail's Spell* won the New York Academy of Science Annual Children's Book Award. Another book, *Hidden Messages*, received the National Science Teacher Award.

Lynne uses technical pens for her drawings. With full color art she adds markers, inks, dyes, watercolors and colored pencils to the black lines. Ms. Cherry attributes her study of woods and forests to her development as an illustrator of animals and nature. Her latest book *The Great Kapok Tree*, is a fine example of her technique and talent.

Projects

- Research and find out the meaning of free-lance, paste-up artist, retail advertising, technical pens, and black lines.

- Invite an artist to visit the class and demonstrate different techniques such as watercolors and inks.

- Have students figure out the ages of the authors. Have them find out how much younger they are than the artists.

- Write a class letter to the author explaining what projects your class is doing based on their book. Thank the author for writing the book!

- Do an art lesson based on the author's technique (see page 64 for suggestions).

Illustrators' Art Projects

Introduce students to some new art techniques and help them get a feeling for methods employed by the authors of *The Wartville Wizard* and *The Great Kapok Tree*. Two projects are outlined below.

Watercolors

Materials: Black marking pens (fine point and broad line); watercolors; white drawing paper

Directions:

- Have the students use various pens to draw an interesting design on the drawing paper. Use curved and straight lines to create an unusual pattern.

- Direct them to watercolor some of the spaces in the design; leave others uncovered.

- Tell students to write a title for their pictures. In small or whole groups have them explain their titles to the others.

"Flashback"

An Abstraction

Materials: Art tissue torn into pieces; large sheet of white paper; paintbrushes; empty margarine cups; water; black markers.

Directions:

- Have students fill their margarine cups half full with water.
- Tell them to dip their brushes into the water and brush the white paper with water.

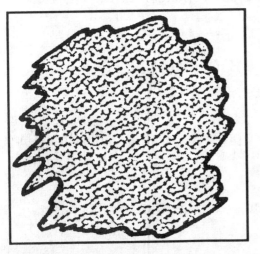

- Direct them to place a piece of tissue onto the wet paper and brush over the tissue with water.
- Have them continue to place pieces of tissue onto the paper, overlapping the pieces and brushing with water.
- Remove all the tissue and let the background dry.
- Draw designs, shapes, etc. onto the background.

64

Musical Ideas

The following ideas and projects can easily be incorporated into the environment thematic unit. Use the Request Letter (page 77) to obtain any necessary supplies. Then follow the directions and add your own ideas, too.

Easy Listening

As a class listen to Camille Saint-Saens' "The Carnival of the Animals" or Igor Stravinsky's "The Rite of Spring." Have the children make up their own body movements to match the mood of the songs. Let the children paint an abstract picture after they have listened to the music. Brainstorm a list of words inspired by the music; use the list of words to write poems.

Sing a Song

Teach students the words and melody to "The Animal Fair" (A copy can be found in *Tom Glazer's Treasury of Songs for Children*, Doubleday, 1964. rev. ed. of *Treasury of Folk Songs*). Illustrate it with a class mural. Substitute forest animal or ocean animal names for the jungle animals listed in the song.

Music Makers

Make your own musical instruments (see suggestions below). Divide students into small groups. Assign each group a different topic, e.g. jungle noises, forest noises, ocean animals noises, etc. In turn, have each group perform an original composition for the class; see if the others can determine the names of the animals and/or environment.

Soft Drink Bottle Horn

Gently blow into the top of an empty soft drink bottle to produce a hollow sound.

Sandy Blocks

Wrap and tape sandpaper around two wood blocks. Gently rub them together.

Milk Carton Rattle

Clean a half-pint milk carton. Put a handful of dried peas or beans in the carton; staple shut. Shake to make a rattling sound.

Coffee Can Drum

Use any size coffee can (empty) with a plastic lid. Drum sticks can be pencils, straws, fingers, brushes, etc.

Encourage the students to invent their own musical instruments and to experiment with the different sounds the instruments can make.

Environmental Desserts

The two recipes below are fun projects to include in your studies of the environment. Dirty Dessert correlates well with *The Wartville Wizard* while Crazy Salad seems especially appropriate for use with *The Great Kapok Tree*. Both are delicious and easy to prepare.

Dirty Dessert

Equipment: Electric or manual beater; mixing bowl; large glass cake sheet; spatula; spoon; ice cream cones

Ingredients: Instant chocolate pudding (enough for one serving per student); milk; chocolate cookies broken into pieces; tiny marshmallows; chocolate chips.

Directions:

- Make the pudding as directed; pour into the cake sheet.
- Stir in the remaining ingredients (use any amount desired).
- Scoop into ice cream cones and serve!

Crazy Salad

Equipment: Knife; 1 large and 1 small mixing bowl; spoon; toothpicks; ladle; foam egg cartons separated into single cups (one per student); measuring cups and spoons.

Ingredients: Fresh tropical fruits (pineapple, papaya, mango, kiwi, banana, etc.); poppy seeds; honey; salad oil; sugar; dry mustard; salt; vinegar; onion juice; cashews nuts (optional)

Directions:

- Cut up the fruits; mix together in the large bowl.
- In the small mixing bowl, mix together the ingredients to make the poppy seed dressing (see recipe below).
- Ladle a small amount of dressing into each egg cup.
- The children can choose fruit from the large bowl using their toothpicks and then dip the fruit into the dressing.
- Sprinkle with cashews, if desired.
- **Variation:** Make fruit kabobs. Cut the fruit into chunks. Alternate different kinds of fruit on a wooden stick. Roll in flaky coconut for a decorative—and delicious—touch.

Poppy Seed Dressing

Mix 3/4 cup (190 mL) sugar, 1 tsp. (5 mL) each of dry mustard and salt, 1/3 cup (85 mL) vinegar, and 1 tblsp. (15 mL) onion juice. Slowly add 1 cup (250 mL) salad oil and beat until thick.

Ecology Games

Use these movement ideas and games wherever they are most appropriate in your environment unit. They require little preparation and equipment yet provide learning fun for your youngsters.

Animal Pantomimes

On separate index cards write the names of the animal characters from the *The Great Kapok Tree*. Give one card to a child and tell him to pantomime that animal for the class. Whoever guesses correctly gets to pantomime the next animal.

Squiggle Like a Snake

Direct the children to squiggle like a snake, flit like a butterfly, lumber like a sloth, or buzz like a bee. Encourage the students to use whole body movements.

Wartville Wizard Tag

This game can be played similarly to the old favorite, Tag. Choose one child to be the Wizard ("it") and give the Wizard a candy wrapper with a piece of double-sided tape on it. In order to get someone out, the Wizard must attach the candy wrapper to another player. The newly-tagged person now becomes the Wizard.

My Tree

To play this outdoor game you will need blindfolds for half the number of players. Pair the students and blindfold one child in each pair. Have everyone begin at the same starting point. The blindfolded players are led by their partner to a tree. Direct the blindfolded players to become familiar with "their" tree by touching it, smelling it, putting their arms around it, etc. Then the blindfolded players are led back to the starting point. Remove the blindfolds and tell the students to find "their" trees. Play the game again with the partners switching roles.

Trash Relay

Form three or four equal-numbered teams. Place a bag of trash items (empty cereal boxes, plastic containers, milk cartons, etc.) in front of each line and an empty bag at the end of each line. Put the same number of items in each bag as there are team members. Tell the first student in each row to take a trash item when the signal to begin is given. Have them pass the trash overhead to the person behind them. The other team members pass the item in the same manner. When it reaches the last person in line, he drops the trash into the bag behind him and runs up to the front of the line. There he begins passing another piece of trash. Play continues until one team has passed back all of its trash.

Talking Big Books

Students will enjoy this multi-media approach to making Big Books. The result is a delightful audio-visual display that is perfect for sharing with an audience of parents or schoolmates. Directions are given below and alternate suggestions for equipment, use, and presentation are provided.

Materials: Tape recorder or VCR; poster board (23" x 29"/59 cm x 72 cm); props for storytelling (see suggestions on page 70); art supplies including paints, fabric scraps, yarn, toothpicks, buttons, construction paper, rickrack, foil, plastic wrap, chalks, watercolors, wrapping paper, newspaper, etc.

Directions:

Note: If the students are inexperienced with writing innovations, model the process with the whole group (see page 69 for complete directions). For those familiar with the process, follow the directions beginning below.

- Divide the students into groups of four or five. Direct each group to choose a story they have enjoyed in the environment unit (*The Wartville Wizard, The Great Kapok Tree,* etc.) .

- Tell them to write an innovation of their chosen story.

- After the story has met with teacher approval, have students write a chunk of text on each large sheet of tagboard.

- Illustrate the text with a variety of materials (for some art ideas see page 64).

- After the book has been prepared, the students can work on sound effects for their story.

- Direct the students to rehearse their text and sound effects together. When they are satisfied with the results, tape record it altogether.

- To present the story, have the students rehearse presenting the tagboard illustrations to go along with the tape recording. Two students at a time can show an illustration.

- Then two other students can hold up the next illustration. Proceed in the same manner until the story is completed.

- Invite parents, the principal, or other classrooms to enjoy your Talking Big Books.

- This project can be completed as a whole class rather than in small groups. Rehearsals can be videotaped and shown to students for self-critiquing. The final Talking Big Book can be displayed on the classroom walls or compiled into books for the classroom library.

How to Write an Innovation

Innovations can be created from poems, stories, or books by substituting nouns, verbs, and adjectives to fit a new context. For example, if the original story is set in the jungle, an innovation could be written about the oceans. Different animal names and descriptive words would be substituted to reflect the new setting. Model the process with the students until they become comfortable with it and can write one on their own or with minimal supervision.

Step by Step Directions

1. As a whole group, decide on one story to innovate. (For the purposes of this example, *The Great Kapok Tree* will be used.)

2. Discuss the setting of the story (the Amazon rain forest). Once the setting has been established, brainstorm other settings. Vote on one to use for the innovation. (For the purposes of this example, the ocean will be used.)

3. Brainstorm lists of ocean words—animals, plants, sounds, descriptive words and phrases, etc. Use these words to replace specified words in the text.

4. The Great Kapok Tree Puzzle on page 37 provides a simplified text to use in this activity. Write the sentences in correct sequence on the chalkboard or overhead projector.

5. Rehearse innovations of the title: "The Gigantic Kelp Bed." One sentence at a time, make changes in each sentence. For example, *The **boa** told how the **tree** was his home.* Changing the bolded nouns might produce, *The **otter** told how the **kelp bed** was his home.* Continue until all lines have been changed.

6. Divide the students into groups and assign them a specific amount of text. You can write the text for them or they may copy the text themselves onto a sheet of paper. Direct them to illustrate their text. Compile the pages to make a Big Book or display the pages on the walls.

The otter told how the kelp bed was his home.

The sea urchin told how he gets his food from the kelp bed.

Helpful Hints

The suggestions below will help you get started with art ideas and sound effects for the Talking Big Books. Encourage students to invent their own methods.

Art

 Paint a brown tempera paint splotch on the paper. Glue toothpicks or craft sticks on the brown body to make a porcupine.

 Draw the outline of a monkey or gorilla. Cut out and glue brown corduroy, felt, or corrugated paper to fit on the outline. Add store-bought moveable eyes (available at craft stores).

 Dye rice, egg shell pieces, or macaroni with egg-decorating kits. After the rice, egg shells, or macaroni have dried, glue the pieces to a shape or outline drawn on the story page.

 Glue macaroni (assorted shapes), rice, beans, seeds, etc. to an outline or shape to make a mosaic or textured picture.

 Cut ribbon, string, yarn, patterned wrapping paper, and rickrack into small pieces. Glue to the surface of a shape or outline.

 For realistic-looking plants, glue actual leaves and petals or artificial flower parts to a shape.

 Dip a sponge into poster paint and go over an outline shape for a mottled effect.

Sound Effects

- Crumple, wave, or tear sheets of newspapers to produce different effects.
- Rub a wooden spoon across the face of a grater.
- Fill glasses with varying amounts of water. Tap gently with a spoon.
- Stomp feet or clap hands on a tabletop to simulate footsteps.
- Experiment with various musical instruments, both commercial and homemade (wooden spoons and lids of pans; aluminum pans and pie plates; empty oatmeal or potato chip cans, etc.).
- Blow into the end of a box of candy for a trumpet sound.

70

An Ecological Bulletin Board

Objective

Use this bulletin board to introduce and reinforce the concept of recycling.

Materials:

Colored construction and butcher paper; scissors; stapler; newspaper; marking pen

Construction

- Line the bulletin board with butcher paper.
- Reproduce the patterns (pages 72 to 76) onto colored construction paper; cut out.
- Staple the basket to the bulletin board.
- Label the bottom patterns with ways to recycle that item (see page 11); attach to the bulletin board.
- Staple the second copy of each pattern on top of its matching pattern on the bulletin board to make a lift-up flap.
- With marking pen write the word RECYCLE in block letters on the newspaper.
- Cut out the letters individually and attach to the bulletin board background. (The whole word can be cut out in a rectangle, if preferred.)

Extension

To make a recyclable bulletin board, assemble all pieces on a large sheet of tagboard and attach with push pins to a bulletin board or a wall. Use the bulletin board again next school year!

An Ecological Bulletin Board *(cont.)*

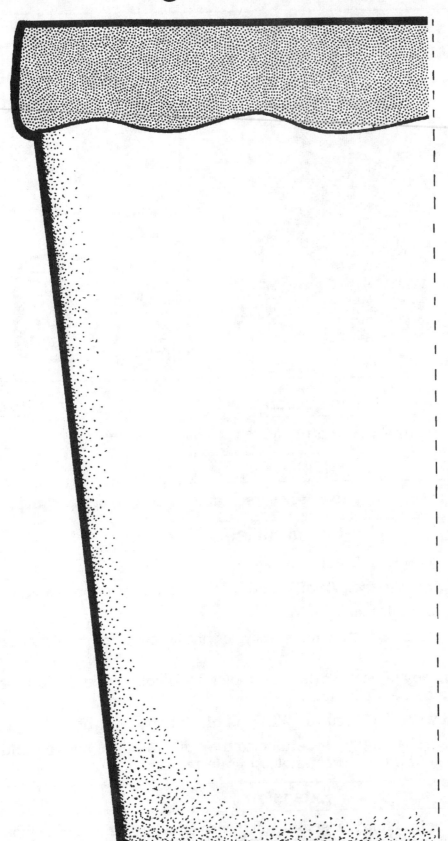

Waste Basket

Attach on top of Tab A (page 73)

72

An Ecological Bulletin Board *(cont.)*

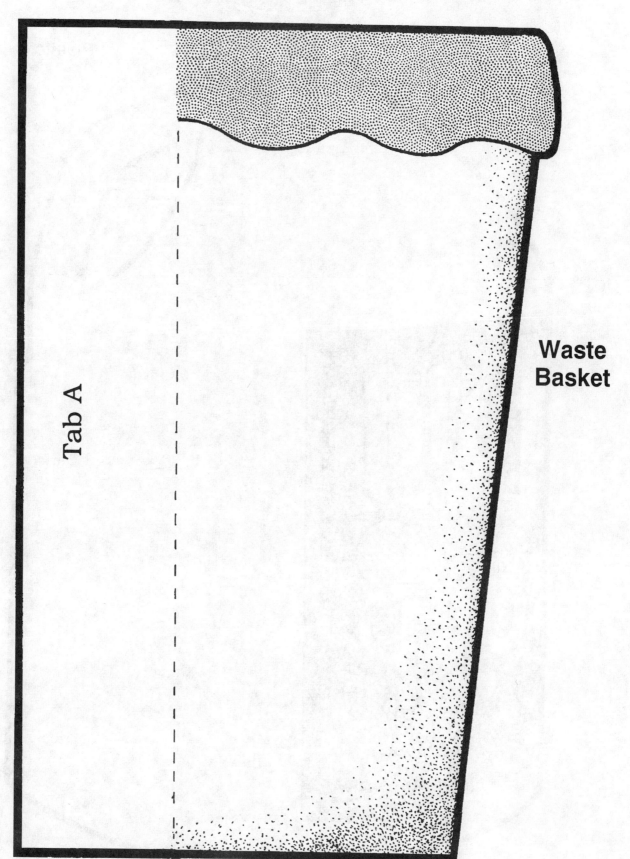

Tab A

**Waste
Basket**

An Ecological Bulletin Board *(cont.)*

Plastic

Make 2.

Cut out

An Ecological Bulletin Board *(cont.)*

Paper

Make 2.

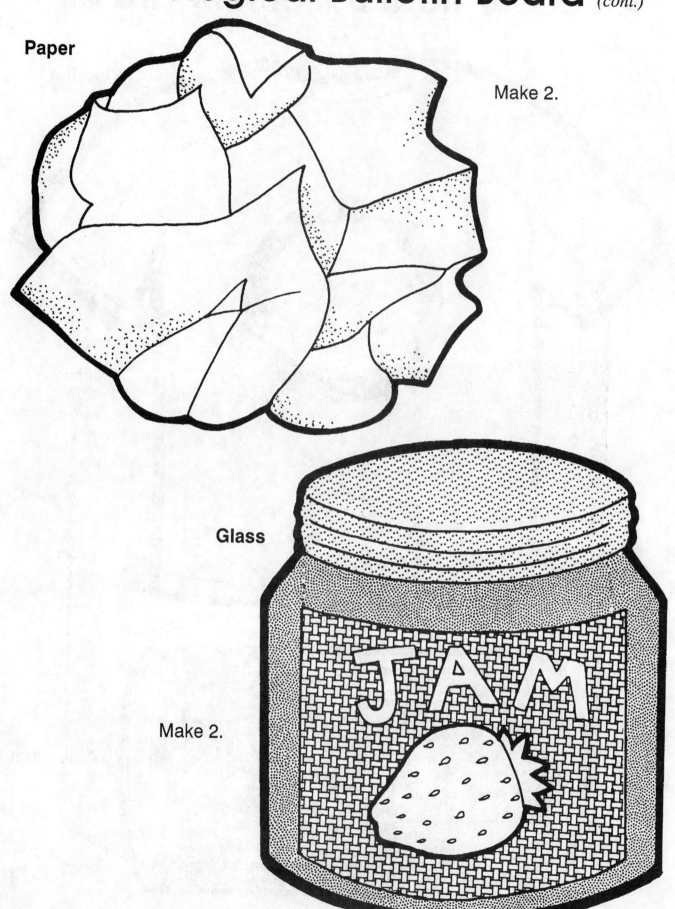

Glass

Make 2.

An Ecological Bulletin Board *(cont.)*

Clothing

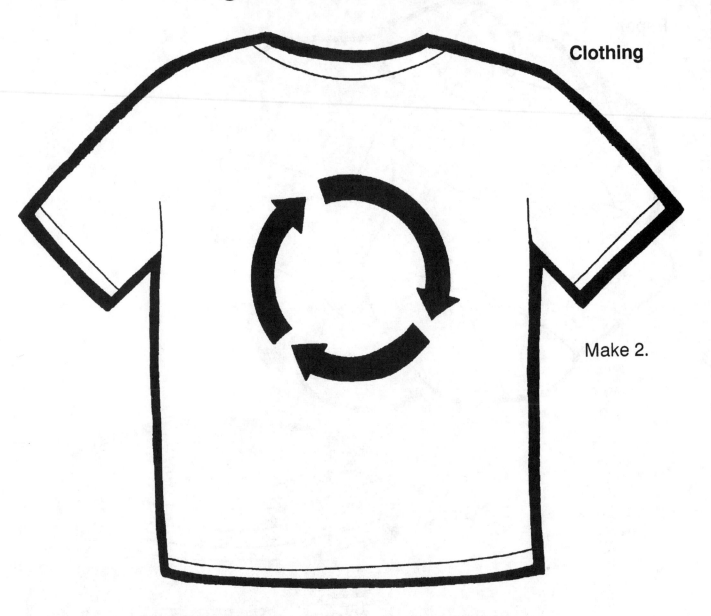

Make 2.

Make 2.

Aluminum

76

Supplies Request Letter

Dear Parents,
As part of the Our Environment unit we will
be _____.
name of project
Each student will need to bring

_____

_____

by _____.
day and date
Also, if you can supply any of the following
items, please send them to school with
your child.

_____

_____

Thank you for your support,
                          Sincerely,

_____
teacher's signature

Wrist Awards

Reward students with these ecology wrist awards. Duplicate onto colored construction paper and cut out. Cut slits on the solid lines. Place the strap around the child's wrist. Tuck the tab into the correct-fitting slit. Fold the tab over to hold the strap in place.

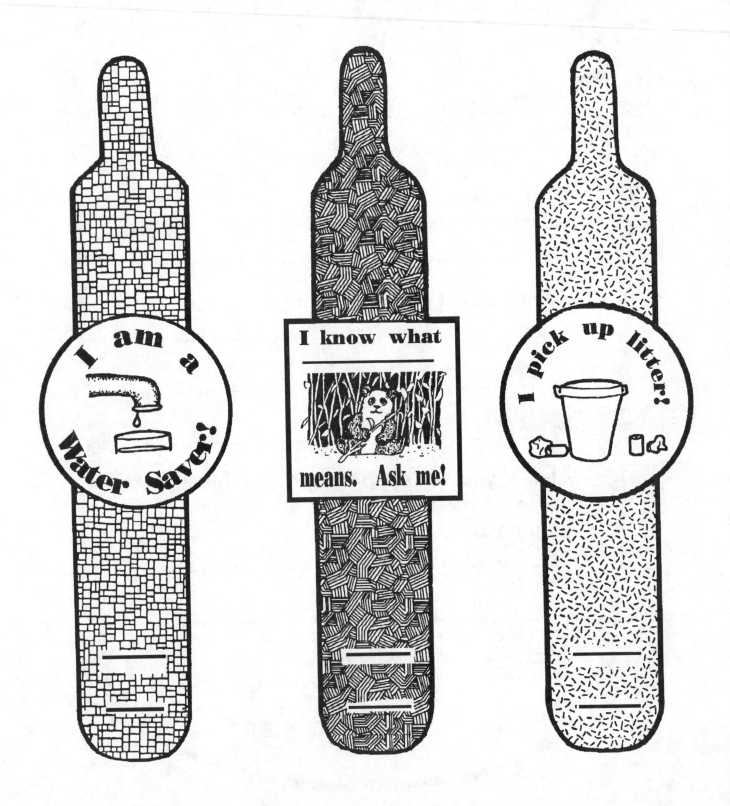

78

Answer Key

p. 17
1. young
2. large
3. short
4. back
5. little
6. messy

pp. 20-21
1. **desert**: cactus, lizard
2. **forest**: owl, pine cone
3. **ocean**: octopus, kelp
4. **plains**: coyote, corn

p. 23
1. 15
2. 13
3. 6
4. 17
5. 5
6. 9

p. 37

p. 38
1. 8
2. 2
3. 6
4. 3
5. 5
6. 4
7. 2
8. 10

p. 45

Tiger: four-legged; has stripes; moves quickly; very big and strong

Sloth: has a smiling face; moves slowly; many plants grow in its fur; lives upside down

Both: live in the jungle; an endangered species

p. 49 - Crossword

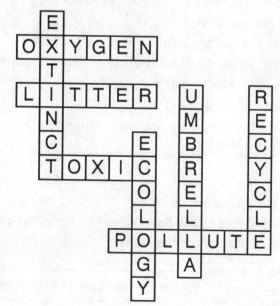

p. 54
1. 4 + 3 = 7
2. 3 + 5 = 8
3. 2 + 4 = 6
4. 5 + 5 = 10
5. 6 + 3 = 9
6. 4 + 1 = 5

p. 55
1. chameleon
2. gorilla
3. python
4. sloth
5. iguana
6. tiger

Bibliography

Fiction

Baker, Jeannie. ***Where the Forest Meets the Sea***. Greenwillow, 1987

Cherry, Lynne. ***The Great Kapok Tree.*** HBJ, 1990

Cosgrove, Stephen. ***Serendipity.*** Creative Education, Inc. 1974

Cowcher, Helen. ***Rain Forest.*** Farrar, 1988

de Paola, Tomie. ***Michael Bird-Boy.*** Prentice-Hall, 1975

Dr. Seuss. ***The Lorax.*** Random, 1971

Madden, Don. ***The Wartville Wizard.*** Macmillan, 1986

Radin, Ruth Yaffe. ***High in the Mountain.*** Macmillan, 1990

Smaridge, Norah. ***Only Silly People Waste.*** Abingdon, 1976

Van Allsburg, Chris. ***Just a Dream.*** Houghton, 1990

Nonfiction

Bash, Barbara. ***Desert Giant: The World of the Saguaro.*** Little, 1990

Cole, Joanna. ***The Magic School Bus at the Waterworks.*** Scholastic, 1988

Desimini, Lisa. ***Heron Street.*** Harper, 1990

Dorros, Arthur. ***Rain Forest Secrets.*** Scholastic, 1990

Earthworks Group, The. ***50 Simple Things Kids Can Do to Save the Earth***. Andrews and McMeel, 1990

Hadingham, Evan and Janet. ***Garbage!*** Simon & Schuster, 1990

Hornblow, Leonora and Arthur. ***Animals Do the Strangest Things***. Random, 1990

Kalusky, Rebecca. ***Help Save Us Sticker Book of Wild Animals.*** Dutton, 1989

Lloyd, David. ***Air.*** Dial, 1982

McGrath, Susan. ***Saving Our Animal Friends.*** National Geographic Society, 1986

Rockwell, Jane. ***All About Ponds.*** Troll, 1984

Showers, Paul. ***Where Does the Garbage Go?*** Harper, 1974

Stewart, Frances Todd and Charles R. III. ***Animals and Their Environments.*** Harper, 1987

Stone, Lynn M. ***Endangered Animals.*** Childrens Press, 1984

Whitcombe, Bobbie. ***Animals in Danger.*** Brimax, 1988

Wood, John Norris. ***Nature Hide and Seek Jungles.*** Knopf, 1987

Poetry

Prelutsky, Jack. (selected by) ***The Random House Book of Poetry for Children.*** Random, 1983

Prelutsky, Jack. (selected by) ***Read-Aloud Poems for the Very Young.*** Knopf, 1986

Silverstein, Shel. ***Where the Sidewalk Ends.*** Harper, 1974

Teacher Created Materials

TCM 283 ***Thematic Unit - Jungle***

TCM284 ***Thematic Unit - Oceans***

TCM 286 ***Thematic Unit - Ecology***

TCM 308 ***Literature Activities for Young Children***

TCM 309 ***Literature Activities for Young Children***